FOR THE WEEKS WE SPEND IN HELL

You are NOT alone

FOR THE WEEKS WE SPEND IN HELL

A Collection of Poetry

By

Mikel Maureé (Mikel Robinson)

Mikel Maureé/For the Weeks We Spend in Hell

ISBN: 979-8-9891384-1-8

Front cover image by Mikel Maureé Robinson, an original acrylic painting entitled,
"The Fire we Fight," from Mikel's personal collection.
Cover Design: Mikel Maureé Robinson
Illustrations: Mikel Maureé Robinson
Editor and Interior Design: Robin D. Hohweiler

Printed by Amazon

Contact the author:
Mikel Maureé Robinson
P.O. Box 2635
Woodward, OK 73802

www.mikelmaureeart.com

ACKNOWLEDGEMENTS

My husband Brett: For loving me out of total darkness and being a creative muse in my life. You lived through these poems with me, even if you don't realize it. And for that I thank you!

Robin D. Hohweiler: To my creative collaborator, how you have encouraged me to grow as a creative and a poet, there is nothing I could ever do to repay you. Thank you!

To my family: Thank you all for always being supportive of my creative journey. It's not always been smooth sailing.

To my many other friends that encourage and support me, you all know who you are.

I also want to acknowledge those of you that don't even know you played a part in the making of this collection, and to all of the life situations that inspired this collection.

Contents

Introduction

It has been exactly one year since I summoned the courage to release my first poetry chapbook into the world. Titled "For the Days We Spend in Hell", it delved deep into the darkest corners of my mind and unleashed words that some may find unsettling or uncomfortable. As I reflect on this past year, I understand that my voice in that first release, and likely in this second one, "For the Weeks We Spend in Hell" won't resonate with everyone. And that's okay.

Initially, I would politely accept when people told me my poetry wasn't their cup of tea. I believed I understood their perspective - after all, my work touches on topics that most people spend their entire lives trying to keep locked away in a cabinet with a double lock to shield their loved ones from the horrors within.

But as time went on and I spoke with many of my readers, something shifted inside of me. I realized that every single human being on this earth shares similar experiences, emotional traumas, crushing feelings, and relentless demons. Some of us can suppress them, for better or worse, and carry on with our lives. Others cannot do so, and it is for those wandering souls I write.

For me personally, this past year has been a journey of emotional growth. Crafting that chapbook and putting it out into the world was one of the wisest, bravest, and most cathartic decisions I have ever made. Strange as it may sound, I am grateful for the painful experiences that inspired much of my work in both works. They have helped me turn a corner and recognize my demons for what they are – just another part of me that a creative mind and a heavy lock can keep at bay.

To any reader who finds solace in my words and sees their own hell reflected in them, please know that you are not alone. You are bigger and more powerful than any demon could ever be. The key is to find your own outlet, whether it be painting, writing, drawing, composing... *creating*. For me, that has been my salvation.

I am humbled and grateful to present this second collection of my work to you. And as always, I welcome and encourage you to reach out to me if I can offer any support or guidance on your journey towards finding light in the darkness.

Mikel
October 31, 2024

My Heart Died

My heart died
To coincide
with the death
already inside.

My heart bleeds
with pride,
I can't stop,
I can't hide,
I'm lonely,
I lied.

My heart's open wide
just peek inside
all you will see is
the miserable
human being
that's caged up
begging to die.

The bleeding colors

mean nothing

the sadness

boiling up

forming bubbles

of nothingness.

My heart died

To coincide

with the love

that's inside.

It meant something

It ended wrong

Though it felt right.

You're meticulous.

You're selfish and

vile inside.

Run and hide.

I won't find you.

Finding you

Means I've died

And I am already

The most

Worthless

Thing

That's alive.

Checkmate

Some people will put you
up on a pedestal
but you'll still find that
you're running from
yourself.

Why are you running dear?
Why does your soul
Feel lost in your skin?

Why do the sounds,
The chatter in your head
Make you dread your existence?

Your life's a chess game
Checkmate.
The End.

Wreck

I am a wreck

I will connect

But I am disconnected

Lost

Walking around with

My eyes shut

My heart wide open

Numb

Connecting to no one

Disconnected from my

Own mind

I am a wreck

Broken promises

Beautiful souls

Sad because

I want it all

Mad because

I have lost control

I am a wreck

Just lose this connection

I am lost with no direction.

No Longer in Fear

I'm broke

I'm shattered

I'm bleeding

And untamed

I'm vibrant

I'm lucid

I'm magic

And enraged

The world is

A wreckage

Of all the things

That I hate

I'm living here

Barely breathing

From the air

That's tainted

From all of the

People who

Don't care

Who they've wasted

No one's in good graces

We're all walking around

With fake faces

The end is near

And I'm no longer

In fear.

Just Never Enough

I just wanted to watch the sunset,

And forget that we all have to live

With our regrets.

I just wanted it to rain,

So, I could wash away

All of this heavy pain.

I just wanted to look at the moon,

And remember how much

I do love you.

Life gets in the way.

I'm torn every day.

I can't stop these thoughts

And the stacks of what nots.

But I'm here for it all.

I may break.

I may fall.

But I cared so much

I'm just never enough.

Not Worth It

There's this

Miserable piece of human

That will always

Just live on

Inside me

That's where all these words

Come from

That's how I make sense

Of the nonsense

That's rambling

Up there inside of me.

I can't stop it

Nothing I ever do helps

Except writing it out

Allowing it to escape my body

Whence it actually came.

It's not a game

It's an illness

From not doing anything.

It lives alone

Casting stones

At the person

Who wants to remain.

It's a lesson

Don't be selfish

You're not worth it anyway.

The Joy

I am damaged

I cannot have it.

The joy like

Everyone else.

I have shortcomings

I am disconnected

From normality.

I am not like everyone else.

These bad feelings

They plague me,

I am not built

Like everyone else.

This life is messy.

I cannot get healthy,

I am not connecting

Like everyone else.

The thing is

No one really is

Ever like everyone else.

The Anxiety

The anxiety

It is bottled up

Inside of me

It's begging

To get out

To wreck me

With its doubt

I won't let it win

I've trained my mind

To win this

The anxiety

It's real

I can't be logical

When it is here

And it makes

Me so angry

My chest starts

To feel like it is caving

My breath begins to shorten

And the tears being to flow

I know what's happening

I don't have control

These feelings

I know them well

They get me every time

I won't take the medicine

It's a crutch

I'm not broken enough

It may sound crazy

But I want to feel it

To feel what it is

To become its master

It just likes to come back

Differently

I use my words

And this paper

To slay it every time

The anxiety

Has its place

I treat it with grace

And it sometimes

Knows its place

I'm training it

My art lives off it

I guess I just need it

Sometimes.

The Intrusive Thoughts

The intrusive thoughts

Do not ever stop.

They dance in my head

They lie in my bed

They follow me

They play tricks on me

They are everywhere.

The intrusive thoughts

Do not ever stop

They plague me

They weigh on me

They live inside of me

They feel so real

And I feel horrible

To hear what they have to say

To know that they come

From some sad, sorry place

That is brewing inside of me

I wish it was not a part of me.

I am Miserable

I am miserable

Melting away and cynical

Hating my own thoughts

For feeling this way

When there are people that are

In a far worse state.

Depression is funny

It creeps and it crawls

All through your veins

And into your heart.

I am miserable

With a giant smile on my face

I laugh and I joke

Trying to keep the demons at bay.

There is nothing funny

About feeling this way.

There is nothing funny

When the logic's away.

Step into Hell

So long

Farewell

I'll meet you in the morning

Before I step into hell.

Goodbye

For now,

I'll miss you in the evening

Before I step into Hell.

Cesspool of Hate

Why are we living

In a cesspool of hate

And only holding onto

The dead end of fate?

Breaking My Own Fucking Heart

I have got to stop breaking my own fucking heart.

I am malicious and vicious

I am reckless and careless

I have got to stop breaking my own fucking heart.

I am a coward, things devoured

I am a menace

I wish you weren't caught up in this.

I have got to stop breaking my own fucking heart.

I have got to stop taking things apart.

I have got to stop being selfish.

I have got to stop mixing it up.

I have got to stop hurting the people that I love.

I have got to start being better.

If I have hurt you,

I am sorry.

I am hurt too.

But that doesn't make it right,

Run the other way.

I won't ever hold blame.

You have to save yourself,

Or you will end up like me

Breaking

Taking

Using

Abusing

Losing

Confusing

Hating

Waiting

Don't worry about me

I will be fine

I am already dead inside.

Living Off Hate

I am going around

Picking up pieces

Except the pieces

Of myself

I am not who I should be

I am just what the world

Needs me to be

I am drowning in love

And living off hate

I am miserable

I am lonely

I am just looking for a Break.

Logic Can't Explain

The pain comes from everywhere
The pages never turn
The air tastes of honey but the bees
never returned.

I have forgotten what's important
Never giving myself space
The wind sweeps down the plains taking my
Energy from its place.

Robbing me of everything
The space I am at is heavy.
I question God for it being this way
I want to be okay, but this is just something
Logic can't explain.

I am Jekyll and Hyde

The inside of my soul

Is just a really dark hole

That's packed with pain

I am really just vain

If you think you've lost it

You actually just got it

But there's nothing there

It is a dark hole of despair

I'll never be happy

I am just not built that way

I am Jekyll and Hyde

I'll make us both cry

You're all better off without me.

The Decision

Just as I made the decision to love you

I can also make the decision to cut you out

Leave you there in despair

Write you off like you needed me to be soft

Like you needed me to care.

I'll always be there

That's just what you thought

Because that's not the truth

I only needed certain pieces of you

And there you'll be left all alone

In your misery

Bet you wish you'd

Never met me.

Strapped Down

You could just shoot me in the face.

I am so fucking sick of the race

Lock me up, call me insane

But that is how I feel

And it is never the same.

It comes and it goes

It is wild and unknown.

It is a curse

A blessed mess

A crooked neck

Strapped down

Tied to the ground.

Saturday Night

It is Saturday night and

I hear you want to fight.

I am here to make right

But you lost the good fight.

And I hear you cannot stand to lose.

This fire in my heart is burning up the night

And everyone is outing the booze

And I am feeling this blue.

Give Me A Break

Give me a break from the chaos

Give me a break from the noise

You drowned me with your inconsistencies

You drowned me in all of your poise

Give me a break from the nonsense

Give me a break from the confusion

You drowned me in my very own thoughts

You drowned me without any thought

Give me a break from the chatter

Give me a break from the latter

You drowned me with all of your words

You drowned me with your delusions

You're broken, I am shattered, I am losing

Stop looking at me

Stop caring you see

I am wicked

And frankly I am just a recluse

Trying not to use others to feel less of the noose

That is tightening around my soul

I am losing all of my control

So just give me a break

I will soon wake

Feeling like I could be made

Into something that is beautiful

Something that is great

If you could only just give me a break.

I Have Never

I have never worked so hard

And not even got that far

People will come and they will say

You have made it so far, what do you mean?

I am mad because I could be farther

But I let stupid shit bother

To the point that I know I could have been farther

Yet here I am

Working so hard for that dollar

That I lost myself and my scholar

But I have gained so much more knowledge

Of what I do not want

Of what makes me crazy and lose every hand

I have been dealt some shit cards

Life has just got to be hard

For me at least

I cannot write

Without losing my heart

In life

In love

In what makes me not want to rise above

The nonsense

The fakes and the follows

What lies ahead is just me in a bed

Lying there

Waiting to be heard

I do not demand your words

While they will pour out of me

I hope that you see

I am not that lovely

As I once seemed

Fuck off

Be gone

I am looking for reasons

To not feel this numb.

I Am a Monster

I am a monster

Of impending doom

I am the rot

That you do not want to consume.

I am the danger

In a perfect world.

I am the darkness

When all you need is light.

I am the tattered pages

Of your written hate.

I am the bad news

When you are feeling great.

I am the weapon that

You need to destroy.

I am the lesson

That you could not question.

The lesson that

You could not avoid.

I Feel Like Death's...

I feel like death's

The only thing that is left

To free me from these feelings

So I can finally rest.

Dead Things

I have this terrible habit

Of keeping dead things alive.

Most of the time it is only in my mind.

I water the bad habits

I give oxygen to the fire,

And I am just a liar.

I Am Not for Everyone

I am not for everyone

Heck, some days I am not even for me

I sit around having talents

But not a single person wants to see

I will never feel wanted

Because some days I don't even want me

I'm a porcelain doll

With a beautifully painted-on face

My skin soft to the touch

But on the inside

I am a cracked-up mess

About to be shattered

Into a million little pieces

I am not for everyone

And today I am not even for me.

Sleepless in the Fire

I cannot sleep

I am exhausted

I am weak

I bring myself

To me own knees

And I beg and plead

For these feelings to

Subside

But they stay

I imagine them

As patrons

Sitting on bleachers

Watching me grow

Even weaker

Taking out bets

Of Whom I will

End up with next

Watching as I grasp

For air

No one even cares

I try to accept

That I actually

Most possibly

Even deserves this

I sleep

But I don't really

Get rest

My bodies just

Working out all

Of my stress

I wake up in cold sweats

While the dreams

Still haunt me

During my waking hours

Sleep doesn't matter

I am cursed

And no amount of

Sleep will keep me

At east.

I am sleepless

In the fire.

I have worn out

All of my desires.

I Will Admit

I will admit

I am a shit

I am impulsive

And compulsive

I will be useful

And truthful

But I am reckless

I will wear a cute necklace

I will crush all of your dreams

I am just that extreme

You will hate me

I admit

I just need to quit.

About the Author

Mikel Maureé Robinson is the Executive Director of the Plains Indians & Pioneers Museum in Woodward, Oklahoma. A true Midwestern native, she spent her childhood in Wichita and Protection, Kansas and graduated from high school in Coldwater. With a passion for storytelling and art, Mikel went on to earn a Bachelor of Science in Mass Communication from Northwestern Oklahoma State University in Alva.

An accomplished writer, podcaster, photographer, and artist, Mikel's unique perspective shines through in all her artistic ventures. Her writing has been featured in collections and online, while her striking photographs and paintings have been exhibited in galleries throughout Western Oklahoma and Kansas.

Currently residing on an estate with her husband Brett (and a host of cats), Mikel is working on renovating one of the houses into a destination Airbnb. That house was once occupied by a (supposed) practicing witch, adding a touch of mystery to their idyllic home. Together, they continue to create and share their love for art and hospitality with those around them.

More about Mikel and her art can be found on her website www.mikelmaureeart.com

Facebook, Instagram, Twitter & TikTok:
@mikelmaureeart

www.ingramcontent.com/pod-product-compliance
Lightning Source LLC
Chambersburg PA
CBHW060042050426
42448CB00012B/3106